Discover Series
ANIMALES DE OCÉANO

Pez Payaso

Coral

Cangrejo

Pescado Damisela

Delfín

Medusa

Ballena Asesina

Pez León

Langosta

Mahi-Mahi

Tiburón Mako

Moluscos

Pez Globo

Dolar de Arena

Gaviota

Caballo de Mar

León Marino

Conchas Marinas

Caracol de Mar

Tortuga Marina

Concha De Erizo de Mar

Calamar

Estrella de Mar

Pescado Rayado Amarillo Dulces Labios

Pez Tang Amarillo

Make Sure to Check Out the Other Discover Series Books from Xist Publishing:

Published in the United States by Xist Publishing
www.xistpublishing.com
PO Box 61593 Irvine, CA 92602

© 2018 by Xist Publishing All rights reserved
Translated by Victor Santana
No portion of this book may be reproduced without express permission of the publisher
All images licensed from Fotolia
First Spanish Edition

ISBN: 978-1-5324-0697-3   eISBN: 978-1-5324-0698-0

www.ingramcontent.com/pod-product-compliance
Lightning Source LLC
LaVergne TN
LVHW070950070426
835507LV00030B/3475